9000865098

Medicine

Medicine

AMY GERSTLER

 PENGUIN POETS

PENGUIN BOOKS
Published by the Penguin Group
Penguin Putnam Inc., 375 Hudson Street,
New York, New York 10014, U.S.A.
Penguin Books Ltd, 27 Wrights Lane, London W8 5TZ, England
Penguin Books Australia Ltd, Ringwood, Victoria, Australia
Penguin Books Canada Ltd, 10 Alcorn Avenue,
Toronto, Ontario, Canada M4V 3B2
Penguin Books (N.Z.) Ltd, 182–190 Wairau Road,
Auckland 10, New Zealand

Penguin Books Ltd, Registered Offices:
Harmondsworth, Middlesex, England

First published in Penguin Books 2000

1   3   5   7   9   10   8   6   4   2

Page vii constitutes an extension of this copyright page.

LIBRARY OF CONGRESS CATALOGING IN PUBLICATION DATA
Gerstler, Amy.
Medicine / Amy Gerstler.
p.   cm.—(Penguin poets)
ISBN 0 14 05.8924 4
I. Title. II. Series.
PS3557.E735M44   2000
811′.54—dc21   99–054554

Printed in the United States of America
Set in Garamond
Designed by Mia Risberg

FOR MARCUS

He oft finds med'cine who his griefe imparts.

—Spenser

ACKNOWLEDGMENTS

The following people have aided and abetted me in various ways and I would like to thank them:

Bernard Cooper, David Trinidad, Sid and Mimi Gerstler, Tina Gerstler, Tony Cohan, Dennis Cooper, Tom Knechtel, Jane Weinstock, Megan Williams, Judith Moore, Alexis Smith, Brian Tucker, David Stanford, Linda Young, Ira Silverberg, Maurya Simon, Eloise Klein Healy, Maura Stanton, Tom Clark, David Lehman, Paul Slovak, and most especially, Benjamin Weissman.

Poems in this manuscript first appeared in the following magazines, sometimes in slightly altered forms:
American Poetry Review, Art Commotion, Boston Review, Crania, Crazy Horse, Faultline, Fourteen Hills, Gas, Kenyon Review, The LA Weekly, Mike and Dale's Younger Poets, Phoebe, Ploughshares, The Prose Poem, Purple, Quarterly West, Santa Monica Review, Snowflake, Verse, and *The World.*

A section of "Lovesickness" appeared in an artists' book entitled *Past Lives*, a collaboration with Alexis Smith.

Contents

Medicine

PRAYER FOR JACKSON

Dear Lord, fire-eating custodian of my soul,
author of hemaphrodites, radishes,
and Arizona's rosy sandstone,
please protect this wet-cheeked baby
from disabling griefs. Help him sense when
to rise to his feet and make his desires known,
and when to hit the proverbial dirt. On nights
it pleases thee to keep him sleepless, summon
crickets, frogs and your chorus of nocturnal
birds so he won't conclude the earth's gone mute.
Make him astute as Egyptian labyrinths that keep
the deads' privacy inviolate. Give him his mother's
swimming ability. Make him so charismatic
that even pigeons flirt with him, in their nervous,
avian way. Grant him the clearmindedness
of a midwife who never winces when tickled.
Let him be adventurous as a menu of ox tongue hash,
lemon rind wine and pinecone Jell-O. Fill him with awe:
for the seasons, minarets' sawtoothed peaks,
the breathing of cathedrals, and all that lives—
for one radiant day or sixty pitiful years.
Bravely, he has ventured among us, disguised
as a newcomer, shedding remarkably few tears.

TO A YOUNG WOMAN IN A COMA

You haven't gulped down your allotted portion
of joy yet, so you must wake up. Recover,
and live to bear children—a girl and a boy—
twins who kiss in the womb and fox trot
on your bladder shortly before they're born.
Find your way back to us. Landmarks include
the lines on your mother's pierced earlobes,
jagged crags of your boyfriend's chipped tooth.
Come up from the basement. Climb those damp
plank stairs and reenter the squinty glare
of consciousness. Grip the rickety handrail.
Go slowly, past jars streaked with mushroom
dust and enriched mud from the house's bowels.
Let your name be written in orange marmalade
across the breakfast table. Reel in your soul.
Tell it to float back, through the portals
of mouth and nose, into its flesh envelope,
so you may enjoy the privileges of being
flooded with pain, inhaling rank hospital
food fumes and seeing your family's patient,
inescapable faces, too beautiful for words.
Surface, even if it feels like you're crashing
through a plate glass window. There's too much
left undone. We can still smell the out-of-doors
all over you: daffodil bulbs, rye bread
and cider. So wiggle your toes. Groan.
Open those gunky eyes. You need to grow older,
have those babies, try to describe what
the other side was like, go ice skating.

NEARBY

When the spiritual axe fell, did you wake up inside *The White Orchard,*
that snowy van Gogh we both admired? Are you lost in his chilly
idyllic painting, under skies filled with white dots he smeared in
with his thumbs? How dare you. How dare you die. Now you
express an absolute restfulness. A sober way of existing, unlike mine.
A shot of tequila gleams on the table. Its vinegarish drip
gilds my innards—that's my report from the salt mine
of the senses tonight. You're supposed to be a ghost now, living on
in shipwrecked tatters like a shredded sailboat sail; sans dirty linen,
gritty winds, and the bane of shaving every day, which you hated.
Once you began to lose your mind, you wisely refused to shave
or be shaved. You put up surprisingly big fights, and I found
myself glad to see you so vehemently defying your keepers,
including me, as I chased you around with a red and white striped
can of shaving cream. Not that you could run much by then. So.
You've had a fortnight's silence. An autumnal lull. Sat out a break
between quarters in the cosmic basketball game. Come back
as a crawfish, a leek, a handful of gravel hens ingest to use as teeth,
a fake preacher who can't control his wolfish streak. I don't care
what you wear. But come back soon. Not seeking revenge
or relief, to which you're mightily entitled, but to meet your new
darkhaired niece and answer a few routine questions.

THE BEAR-BOY OF LITHUANIA

Girls, take my advice, marry an animal. A wooly one is most consoling. Find a fur man, born midwinter. Reared in the mountains. Fond of boxing. Make sure he has black rubbery lips, and a sticky sweet mouth. A winter sleeper. Pick one who likes to tussle, who clowns around the kitchen, juggles hot baked potatoes, gnaws playfully on a corner of your apron. Not one mocked by his lumbering instincts, or who's forever wrestling with himself, tainted with shame, itchy with chagrin, but a good-tempered beast who plunges in greedily, grinning and roaring. His backslapping manner makes him popular with the neighbors, till he digs up and eats their Dutch tulip bulbs. Then you see just how stuffy human beings can be. On Sundays his buddies come over to play watermelon football. When they finally get tired, they collapse on heaps of dried grass and leaves, scratching themselves elaborately, while I hand out big hunks of honeycomb. They've no problem swallowing dead bees stuck in the honey.

A bear-boy likes to stretch out on the floor and be roughly brushed with a broom. Never tease him about his small tail, which is much like a chipmunk's. If you do, he'll withdraw to the hollow of some tree, as my husband has done whenever offended since he first left the broad-leafed woodlands to live in this city, which is so difficult for him. Let him be happy in his own way: filling the bathtub with huckleberries, or packing dark, earthwormy dirt under the sofa. Don't mention the clawmarks on the refrigerator. (You know he can't retract them.) Nothing pleases him more than a violent change in climate, especially if it snows while he's asleep and he wakes to find the landscape blanketed. Then his teeth chatter with delight. He stamps and paws the air for joy. Exuberance is a bear's inheritance. He likes northern light. Excuse me, please. His bellow summons me.

Let me start again. True, his speech is shaggy music. But by such gruff instruction, I come to know love. It's difficult to hear the story of his forest years with dry eyes. He always snuffs damply at my hand before kissing it. My fingers tingle at the thought of that sensitive, mobile nose. You've no *idea* how long his tongue is. At night, I get into bed, pajama pockets full of walnuts. He rides me around the garden in the wheelbarrow now that I'm getting heavy with his cubs. I hope our sons will be much like their father, but not suffer so much discomfort wearing shoes.

THE NATURALIST'S WIFE

He was a stricken puritan when we met,
a bit of prude and a clod. I saw his snapshot
in the family album, as a kid, grinning,
the skeleton of a prehistoric horse sprawled
at his feet. He had a condor egg in each hand,
and he held them, even at age ten, as though
they were the breasts of his beloved. Why
this picture made me mad to have his hands
on *me* is anybody's guess. He looked a bit like
a newly hatched cuckoo, with his funny jutting
tufts of hair. After he became famous,
on his birthday each year, a Swiss rabbit fancier
would send him a crate of rare hares. The first
time he kissed me he prefaced the peck
by wondering aloud: "Now, how many bees
have visited this little flower?" I twisted the sprig
of mistletoe he'd given me and whispered
under my breath, "Far too few." I did resent
some of the sights I was later privy to—
such as his sketches of a dead elephant's
stomach contents. During the third or fourth
year of our marriage a strange revolution
took place, and for a while, the government
of his tongue was overthrown. That was hard
to bear. Our sixth-born son (the co-discoverer
of oxygen and of a breed of green lizards
who pose for photographs when the weather
turns warm) journeyed far and wide,
like his father, slept in fossil beds,
adapted to dark caverns and practiced oratory

at the seashore. But he wrote me each week,
homesick for the whistle of my dented copper
kettle and the reek of my heartsease tea. Who
stands the chance of living the longest? The unhappy
salamander pinched in the heron's big, tweezery
beak is offended by the question, which I
therefore withdraw. My husband willed his library
to an untaught wildman from the woods.
It included a volume of essays about dew,
a monograph on what clings to the feet
of migratory birds and the autobiography
of a squid named William. My husband,
fingers sticky with pinfeathers and speckled
with ink stains, has been dead these ten years.
When we are reunited, in heaven, or purgatory,
or at some bird sanctuary, or on an overgrown river-
bank (I really don't care where), I know he'll still
be obsessed with finding out why different varieties
of gooseberries vary in hairiness. Hand in hand,
we'll perch on a low branch and watch a tree full
of weasels hissing and showing their teeth.

Yom Kippur in Utah

Come sit in the absolving shade of a plane tree
and contemplate the forgiveness you crave.
Lists of sins you committed during the past year
are whispered back into existence. They sift
into consciousness, surprised at all the attention
they're getting, shy as mice and houseflies
who find themselves canonized. You haven't
done enough for anyone you love. You've
neglected your parents. You spend eons sleeping.
You're envious of everyone—your silent
father, puttering around in the garage,
assembling ships in bottles, his beard
white as a christening gown. Even the squeaky
front door makes you want to trade places:
it opens and closes so easily. Now, out of nowhere,
it's snowing. Broken white lines slant across
your visual field. Sloppy, sleety blobs splat
on shake roofs, streak the smoke-darkened
brickwork of Victorian homes that rule
this part of town, just south of the graveyard.
Long, grassy and partly unfenced, the cemetery's
arranged by faiths. Jewish section, Catholic area,
the Christian hills—all with separate entrances.
Each plot boasts its own address. Pink
or dark marble stones decorated with roses,
praying hands, crosses or stars (a young boy's
marker is chiseled with dinosaurs) preserve
curious names like Wilfred, Adeline, Barnett—
solid citizens who knew the virtue of eating
three big home-cooked meals each day.

or a church elder wearing Dad's brand of aftershave—
a bracing, South Sea island scent favored by
that kind-eyed, grizzled man who sired you,
who likes to eat sauerkraut with tiny meatballs,
whom you love along unseeable frequencies
as he wipes his mouth with a white napkin
and urges you to confess everything.

These upright neighbors' titles *belong*
on granite slabs, in pretty typefaces
with lilting flourishes at the ends of letters. Be
positive and philosophical when confronted
with pain, they say. Sleep in Jesus. Sleep
in belief. The Mormons here can convert you
even after you've passed away. That's how much
they care about your salvation. Did the past,
that greased but creaky machine, hum along
to a more complex rhyme scheme than ours?
Were its griefs worthier, more ornate,
better attended? Were our dead elders
read to sleep more completely? Were they
better versed—supplied with richer texts
mourners felt embedded in as they sipped
home-brewed oblivion at wakes? Or were
our forebears' sufferings just as blunted,
obscured by the billowing scrims of religion
and tight-lipped denial, their spirits struck dumb,
cinched in by belts, girdles and trusses? The snow
downgrades to rain. It pinstripes the glittery
windows. There's a bright line in the latest MRI
of your brother's skull. Is that some kind of shining
path too? He's on his way to the Cayman Islands
to go diving. Fish hang in the clear water, festive
as Christmas ornaments: crimson and gold, orange
and lime green. Puffers, rockfish and rays wait
as he struggles into his wet suit to enter their element.
And what on earth are you doing in Utah, so far
from your duty, where it's believed dead spinsters
and stillborn infants wed in heaven? Here below,
in the realms of honey and mud, steeples snag
the sky. The air smells serious and holy as a felon

THE STORY OF TOASTED CHEESE

Toasted cheese hath no master.
—a proverb

Toasted cheese hath no master.
Streams of priests running
from pink bungalows faster
and faster were seen reading
The Fronds of God,
prophesying disaster.
Indoors, toddlers munched crumbs
of ancient wall plaster.
You slapped her for calling Dad
a "majestic bastard"?
At the mouth of a sacred cave,
kneeling in gravel, he asked her.
The ostrich race will take place
in that picturesque cow pasture.
Will you have the oysters Rockefeller
now to begin your repast, sir?
Her premonition consisted
of "seeing" her dear sister
romanced by a sandblaster.
Monique loved the rough, comforting
hum of that scruffy black cat's purr.
The botanist finally recognized
(tears filling her overworked eyes)
a rare, blue, Chinese aster.

A Nautical Tale

Her jailer and her tailor posted bail.
But a sailor stole the mailer
containing the ill-fated payment
from the safe in the bondsman's trailer,
tripping over a low railing
around the trailer park's carp pond
as he made his hasty escape.
His shipmates always joked
that the old salt had an ocean-soaked
peach pit for brains, or maybe a caper,
and that this short shrift upstairs
(which untold cruel years at sea
worsens rather than repairs)
accounted for his twisted, driftwood-gray
malaise as well as his famous lack
of restraint. Lifting her skirts
and her bail, he kidnapped the burglaress
in question, leaving a trail
of barnacle shells and tattered writs.
On board, the crew, drunk and groping
for their wits, heard her salivate
under her gag, as the whaler breasted
choppy waters. Finally he untied her,
amidships, seized her by the hips
and roughly kissed her peppery lips,
while the cabin boy (also a kidnap victim),
screamed repeatedly, "Y'all better call me
Mister!" Weeks later, by the time

they'd reached the island chain,
the female thief was frailer,
and those nail holes in the cabin boy's hands
and feet had healed into typical blisters.

Loss

The world cowers and draws away from you.
Lisping rivers whisper watery rumors,
like *Your dad's in jail, but he'll be back*
for Christmas, armed to the teeth.
A friend finds himself suffering
unbearable facial pain. Another man
you admire was warned by his team of MDs
that any attempt at sex could cause
a massive heart attack. The bird perched
on this drainpipe gargles his song
so rustily he seems to be a pip-squeak
machine—feathers fake, gizzard full
of tiny gears. You can still smell
the brimstone from last night's
refinery fire on the streets this morning.
Sadness inhabits your every cell.
It erupts from pores, your new perfume.
The brave few who draw close to you
are treated to a quick whiff:
part eau de regret, part ruined brewery.
Half the planet away, a volcano's
spitting up rocks big as trucks,
then vomiting columns of water
from the lake that's been stuck
down its throat since it was formed.
Maybe you can relate to the volcano's pain.
I'd like to erect a monument
to all loves lost to me. Building
materials would be blocks of lava,
and things that start with the letter "G"—

gunnysacks, glassworms and gingersnaps,
for instance, plus dozens of bottles
of grappa Dad left moldering
in the basement when he lit out
for a crime spree. I'd also decorate
my memorial with these green gems
he hid behind the false wall in his closet,
in that trunk covered with obscene graffiti.
Oh, he'll never come home.
Thank goodness it rains occasionally,
or there'd be no hope of breeze,
pardon, relief. Everything's dripping . . .
and a milliliter of comfort's wrung
from each plink of water into more water,
like coins jingling in the pockets
of the bodiless, who no longer need them.

An Attempt at Solace

Thin ribbons of fear snake bluely through you like a system of rivers. We need a cloudburst or soothing landscape fast, to still this panic. Maybe a field of dracaena, or a vast stand of sugar pines—generous, gum-yielding trees—to fill our minds with vegetable wonder and keep dread at bay. Each night before we sleep, grazing animals file soundlessly by us, with kind looks in their eyes. Their calm, accepting expressions crowd out darker images that buzz and swarm as if our pillowed heads were beehives.

Even the monks I studied were in sore need of comfort. They considered themselves inmates, bit their sooty fingernails to the quick. I often caught them sobbing at dusk, terrified of each sunset's accompaniment, an adverse fate they heard oompah-ing up over the horizon like infernal tuba music.

Everyone we love's under constant threat. A blood-smeared boat's anchored in the Gulf of Mexico, motor still running. The virus decimates our ranks unchecked. Its victims must choose between madness and blindness. The aged, whose natural heat begins to fail them, flail and rave, uncomforted. Physicians continue to nod off during surgeries. Flies zoom through sickrooms, loud as prop planes.

It's not raining regular rain. These droplets are greasy, and they burn. All the frogs are long gone. Are we just paper dolls or pencil sketches to our maker, to be snipped apart or painted away at whim? We fell asleep last night in each other's arms. This morning we wake in a strangely decorated classroom. Sitting erect at uncomfortable desks, restless as wild guinea pigs, we see our would-be teacher swallow pill after pill made of dried, ground-up spiders.

SCORCHED CINDERELLA

This sooty beauty can't yet shed light.
But soon she'll exude a myopic glow
even our cynical paperboy won't be immune to.
Her little hands are cold as Saturn.
She has the accusing eyes of some dying
feline. Her unfettered mind grinds like
a sawmill, or it tinkles like chandeliers
breezes are fingering. She ignites
ne'er-do-wells and solid citizens
alike. She demanded we tattoo an axe
and a skull on her pelvic girdle:
guideposts for explorers hoping to plant
their flags in her lost continent.
Her hair's a forest of totem poles.
Her feet, scentless orchids, cherish
their seclusion in the twin greenhouses
of her heavy corrective shoes. She dines
on hawk wings, beets and unspeakable
custards. How can any of us, daughters
of our mother's disastrous first marriage,
hope to land husbands with her around?
We suffer by comparison with every tick
of the clock. Some say that next to her
we're like stray dogs who scavenge grass
all winter, or quick lizards skittering
along pantry shelves behind dusty pickle
jars. We've locked our sister up, covered
her with tiny cuts. She insists she likes
her hair better since we singed it.
She says people are whispering inside

the air conditioner. It's getting harder
to slap her awake every day to face
the purer girl we're scouring her down to,
but she's still worth a detour,
if you happen to be passing through.

A Non-Christian on Sunday

Now we heathens have the town to ourselves.
We lie around, munching award-winning pickles
and hunks of coarse, seeded bread smeared
with soft, sweet cheese. The streets seem
deserted, as if Godzilla had been sighted
on the horizon, kicking down skyscrapers
and flattening cabs. Only two people
are lined up to see a popular movie
in which the good guy and the bad guy trade
faces. Churches burst into song. Trees wish
for a big wind. Burnt bacon and domestic tension
scent the air. So do whiffs of lawn mower exhaust
mixed with the colorless blood of clipped hedges.
For whatever's about to come crashing down
on our heads, be it bliss-filled or heinous,
make us grateful, OK? Hints of the savior's
flavor buzz on our tongues, like crumbs
of a sleeping pill shaped like a snowflake.

Lovesickness

(a radio play for four disembodied voices)

(Sound fades in, as if being tuned in on a staticky radio)

ED: Love doesn't reside in the heart, anyway. Love resides in the liver along with jaundice.

CONNIE: *(soothingly)* That's right. Throughout all its existence, the body is a house on fire. So banish your eloquence; it will do you no good here.

NOREEN: Just close your eyes and listen to the blaze crackle and roar. Sit back. Get comfortable. In any flesh-and-blood discussion, the agitation of breathing and seeing undermines me. It's a tune I can't shut out.

(She clicks on radio. Soft radio music begins, underneath speech)

NICHOLAS: The sensible world flashes its brightly colored panties at you and all seems lost. You dangle between believing you're angel-food and worm-meat. Then the phone rings and the machine picks it up . . .

NOREEN and CONNIE: *(annoyed, disappointed)* . . . Him again.

ED: The green light flashes, turns red. Passions cool. Ahem. AHEM. Just trying to get your attention. A square of light from the window falls on your arm.

NOREEN and CONNIE: The heat revs up.

ED: It pools and shimmers like a lake. Someone complains on the radio. *(Switch radio from music station to talk)* You rub a clean circle on the smeared window glass with your fist, shade your eyes and peer through. You notice for the first time that day the scenery's bleached white, the color of lunatics and troubled, shy individuals.

(Radio clicked off)

CONNIE: I could hold out no longer.

ED: I could hold out no longer.

NICHOLAS and NOREEN: I can hold out no longer.

(*Short pause*)

NOREEN: Ok. OK. I'm glad you're gone. Now that you're not here, I can do as I like. But I don't mean that at all! I didn't know what I was saying. I wasn't myself back then, just a second ago. I take it all back. What on earth could have come over me?

NICHOLAS: It must have been:

(*Rapidly*):

NOREEN: The antibiotics talking!

CONNIE: Postpartum depression.

ED: The novocaine wearing off.

NICHOLAS: A blood sugar problem.

ALL: (*deliberately*) I was mad at myself, not you.

NOREEN: My bursitis was kicking up.

ALL: (*deliberately*) I got fired.

CONNIE: My stepfather called again and read me the riot act.

NOREEN: I have to appear in court in the morning.

ED: Maybe I slipped into some kind of . . .

NICHOLAS: Valium

NOREEN: Halcyon

CONNIE: aspirin . . .

ED: . . . trance.

(*Slight pause*)

NICHOLAS: Besides, I only said/

(*Rapidly*):

CONNIE: wrote/

ED: thought that crazy stuff . . .

NOREEN. When I was premigraine.

NICHOLAS: During a blackout.

CONNIE: In a fit of insomnia.

NOREEN: After a short, violent rainstorm.

ED: The day before my big deadline.

CONNIE: On the first day of my period.

ED: After I'd been on a juice fast for two weeks.

NICHOLAS: (*deliberately*) I . . . jotted it down on a bar napkin and mailed it while I was still drunk.

(*Pause*)

CONNIE: I love it when you whine like a dog.

NOREEN: I adore it when you salivate audibly.

ED: I love it when the dirty words are in Latin, for instance:

NICHOLAS: *coitus rarissimus, actus quasi masturbatorius, in corpore feminae, sine ulla voluptate.*

(*Music*)

ED: My fingertips buzz, . . .

NOREEN: my skin feels like fur, . . .

NICHOLAS: words drag in my windpipe; . . .

CONNIE: . . . but this could happen to anyone, and how can I possibly be sorry? I'm simply less and less sure of my feeble belief in the soul, and you of all people must know I never qualified as the body's apologist. Let me take you down to the basement, where many of his outcries . . .

ALL: AHH!

CONNIE: . . . and his last gasps . . .

ALL: GASP

CONNIE: . . . are preserved in sealed mason jars that rest on red velvet cushions—it's a sort of informal breath museum. In fact, the lifelike laughter, singing, and swearing you've heard in this house tonight . . .

(*Short radio blast*) . . .

CONNIE: . . . were all produced in the same way. (*Tiny pause*) I hope you know your every respiration means the world to me. Your trachea and glottis are my obelisk and sphinx. Your optic nerve, indeed, each of your . . .

ED, NICHOLAS, NOREEN: (*droning*) . . . One hundred fifteen—odd million rods . . .

CONNIE: . . . and . . .

ED, NICHOLAS, NOREEN: (*droning*) Six-point-five-million cones,

CONNIE: . . . which enable you to perceive . . .

ED, NICHOLAS, NOREEN: (*singing*) . . . light and color,

CONNIE: are precious to me, my apple seed,

NOREEN: my flowering branch,

ED: my shining fork tine,

NICHOLAS: my sugar beet,

ALL FOUR: my nectarine, my alveoli, my Wall of Jericho, my carbon dioxide.

CONNIE: Darling body chemistry: by virtue of your sweetness I am never entirely lost or afraid. Just knock some holes in this darkness big enough for us to stick our heads through and then we can see what the sky's up to tonight.

(*Pause*)

ED: Of all causes, the stars and devotion are the remotest.

(*Music*)

NOREEN: Quiet our illusory and fugitive longings and launch them aloft, Dear Lord. Let them pollute those pure reaches where snow begins its pilgrimage. Just loosen your dry grasp on us, and we promise to mention your name to each other occasionally, and picture you in our minds: . . .

NOREEN and NICHOLAS: . . . a hopelessly skinny figure in robes and a yoga pose. We don't want to love you in that slavish way flies adore beeswax—the monotonous gloss their tiny hairlike legs are stuck knee-deep in. Help us wriggle free, help us discover some other, braver way.

(*Pause*)

ED: Now I see my helplessness most plainly. One set of glands calls out to another, and I'm powerless to remain silent, though after what happened last year, such encounters have lost nearly all their zing, and seem little better than gimmicks, figments, or weak anesthesia to me.

(*Pause*)

NICHOLAS: The idea of entering. There's a threshold, and then you cross it and you're in . . . when is it ever that simple? It's more like never-endingly entering some cheap mystery novel entitled *The Case of the Infinite Portal*, or *The Affair of Eternally Held Breath*, or whatever; a state resembling the nervous sleep of a voiceless boy—without direct expression, without precise confines. Entering is endless, like that fateful Sunday afternoon that just thunders on and on. Like the journey of the womb that wanders through the body like an empty pear, kindling hysteria in its wake but never settling anywhere. To wish to enter is to be homeless and adrift, like the first bird Noah sent out to find dry land when there was none, before the flood waters had receeded, circling . . .

NICHOLAS and NOREEN: . . . and circling . . .

ALL: . . . and circling the drowned earth.

(*Pause*)

CONNIE: His hungry orgasm swallowed them like quicksand. We don't have to say any more . . . you get the gist of it.

(*Slight pause*)

ED: What follows is a list of the motifs of tattoos cataloged on ladies of the night who were arrested in Italy during a one-year period, in descending order of frequency of occurrence:

NICHOLAS: (In other words) An honor roll of the most popular tattoos according to Italian prostitutes!:

CONNIE: —men's names and initials

NOREEN: —men's heads

CONNIE: —the dates and years these women had known certain lovers

NOREEN: —hearts

CONNIE: —the letter "E" after a man's name, signifying eternal love

NOREEN: —funeral crosses

CONNIE and NOREEN: —names of female friends

CONNIE: —birds

NOREEN: —butterflies

CONNIE and NOREEN: —a rose surrounded by leaves

(*Speeding up*):

CONNIE: —ribbons

NOREEN: —a ring

CONNIE: —a ship

NOREEN: —a star

CONNIE: —a flag

NOREEN: —a cannon, and last but not least,

CONNIE: —religious symbols.

(*Slight pause*)

CONNIE and NOREEN: How love is akin to the pain of chaos.

ALL: You are an exceptionally complex devotional image! Wanting your entirety at once, . . .

ED: . . . I still can't keep you in one piece.

CONNIE: Limbs and torso distract from the face, which I need to keep in plain sight. I'd hoped to honor your body as a whole, but it keeps coming apart and rushing at me . . .

NICHOLAS: . . . the uncontrollable confessions of a skeleton:

(*Rapidly*):

NOREEN: . . . hip,

ED: thigh,

CONNIE: lip,

ED: fingernail,

NICHOLAS: the slang of skin . . .

NOREEN: . . . they keep interrupting each other. The columns of the legs. Gnash of teeth, rasp of hair, rough tongue. Where are you in all this urban sprawl? In which district does your essence reside? Then there's your voice: . . .

ED: . . . a newly dug-up, earthy uncertainty,

NICHOLAS: . . . flecked with spit. You become ungainly as a train, problematic as a camel. In our neck of the woods, physicality is but an airborne balloon in search of its pin.

(*Slight pause*)

NOREEN and ED: I won't come unless she does.

(*Very slight pause*)

NOREEN: (*professorial*) He founded modern sexual pathology. As a man, he embodied all of the virtues and none of the failings of the true pioneer. He was the first to explore the possibility that prolonged ungratified desire is responsible for a variety of nervous conditions in both men and women. As his fame grew, letters carrying the most astounding confessions reached his desk. In the few photographs we have of him he looks a bit like our own Herman Melville, with the same thick squarish beard flowing over his shirtfront. Through his hands a succession of . . .

CONNIE, ED, and NICHOLAS: . . . rapists, the undersexed, stranglers,

NICHOLAS: rippers,

ED: stabbers,

CONNIE: necrophiliacs,

ED: sadists, fetishists,

NICHOLAS: cross-dressers, lovers of velvet and fur,

CONNIE: despoilers of children,

CONNIE, ED, and NICHOLAS: practicers of bestiality, exhibitionists, nympho-maniacs, voyeurs and others afflicted by the (alleged) Defects of Love . . .

NOREEN: . . . passed, and unburdened themselves of their stories, the most explicit parts of which he translated into Latin . . .

(*A few bars of music*)

NICHOLAS: *Paranoia sexualis persecutoria, libido insatiata.*

CONNIE: There are as many ways of loving as there are of disposing of the dead.

(*Slight pause*)

NOREEN: Some cures for lovesickness: diet, baths, . . .

CONNIE and NICHOLAS: . . . the aid of saints, . . .

NOREEN: . . . exercise, hearing good news, study, sleep, music, mirth . . .

ED: (*quickly*) . . . herbs purges fasts cordials and elixirs, . . .

NOREEN: . . . leaping from a rock, a change of place, honest labor,

CONNIE, ED, and NICHOLAS: and last but not least,

NOREEN: my personal favorite: bloodletting.

(*Very slight pause*)

CONNIE: A pale dribble of breast milk faintly colors the bathwater. Another swallow of immunity, spiraling down the drain. I don't care what anyone says, the sicker you are, the dearer you are to me. Prepare for bed, prepare for burial. This is my mystical experience and I don't intend to share it with anyone, so keep your grimy paws off. She took a fistful of pins between her lips and said: . . .

NOREEN: . . . kiss me.

CONNIE: Wracked with hysterical laughter he took me in his arms. I see myself as a withered tree—every drop of passionate sadness turns to sap. Are all animals really melancholy after sex? Impalas? The praying mantis?

NOREEN: There's nothing left to defend yourself against.

(*Very slight pause*)

NICHOLAS: I find my desires humiliating—a depleting captivity—evidence that I'm no more than a deluded inmate in a depressing sexual zoo. My solution? I prefer not to participate, to impose instead the strictest rule over myself and the situation, to watch antics staged for my distant and delayed stimulation from some safe hidden place, say, a tiny peephole bored through the closet door.

ED: We are but toys, little jointed wooden men, and must conduct ourselves accordingly—mustn't babble and rave but seem grateful in ambulation, speech, and apprehension.

NICHOLAS: Some nights I prefer to exhaust myself intellectually, falling asleep in the library with my cheek on a well-thumbed page, on that fold-out illustration of an uncorrupted face, a pure neck, a pile of uninsistent flesh which I kiss and then taste the pasty flavor of low-grade paper on my lips.

(Slight pause)

NOREEN: The list of foods that may incite lovesickness includes: strong wine, pepper, leeks, onions, pine nuts, sweet almonds, syrups, snails,

ED and NICHOLAS: the testicles of animals,

NOREEN: and eggs.

(Very slight pause)

ALL: Enough! Fan no more the flame that consumes me. I can hold out no longer.

(Slight pause)

ED: Let me show you something. This is the face of a woman who killed her children. This is the upper lip of a virtuous spinster. This is the armpit of a white male artist who became fascinated with black male nudes and was unjustly reviled for it.

NICHOLAS: There is the forehead of a plagiarist.

CONNIE: Here we have the downy cheek of a baby with a high fever.

NOREEN: This nose belonged to an animal lover.

ED: This is the hairline of a man who thought he could turn himself into a wolf. Here is the necknape of a belly dancer. This is the left hand of a woman whose blood boils when I touch her.

CONNIE: This is the navel of a lady who once made it hail by staring at the sky severely.

NOREEN: Here is the smile of a child who has been given a sedative.

NICHOLAS: These are the knees of a man addicted to champagne.

CONNIE: Here we see the clubby fingers of a boy who's alive today due solely to the strength of his will.

NOREEN: Here we have the right collarbone of a man of meekness.

NICHOLAS: There is the instep of a woman of the world.

ED: Here is the tongue of a man who lives by his charm alone. This is the wrist of a mother-to-be who is carrying triplets. Here is the cellist's buttock I've been promising you for so long. And last but not least: here's your tooth I knocked out that day years ago. I've been saving it to return to you on just such a joyous, grave occasion as we find ourselves surrounded by today. Put out your hand, and I'll place in your palm that fateful incisor, that tiny white accusation.

(End)

THE BRIDE GOES WILD

You Can't Run Away from It and You Can't Take It
With You, Man of a Thousand Faces: The Children
Upstairs, Brats; All These Women Up in Arms—
Misunderstood Husband Hunters. It Started in Paradise—
The Best of Everything: Ten Nights in a Bar Room, Men
Without Names, The Exquisite Sinner High and Dizzy—
Long Legs, Dimples, The Velvet Touch. Foolin' Around,
Just This Once, She Had to Say Yes. A Night to Remember.
Don't Tell. I Confess—I'm No Angel, I Am the Law!
The Fiend Who Walked West, Breathless, Accused
My Foolish Heart. The Pleasure of His Company
Changes White Heat to a Cold Wind in August.
But One Night in the Tropics, I Saw What You Did.
Ready, Willing and Able, Naughty but Nice, She Wore
a Yellow Ribbon. Miles from Home, Living It Up,
She Couldn't Say No—My Sister Eileen—Too Young to Kiss,
Each Pearl a Tear. The Awful Truth: Ladies Love Brutes.
The Good News: The Devil Is a Sissy. So Tickle Me,
Doctor X, Truly Madly Deeply. Keep Laughing. You Gotta
Stay Happy. Naked, the Invisible Woman Cries and Whispers
Nothing but the Truth, Too Scared to Scream.

OVERHEARD AT THE WATERING HOLE

What were my virtues?
Where did they migrate?
Have they enveloped budding
shrubs like dozens of coupling
butterflies? Or settled
in some dense, thorny forest?
Maybe they sought refuge
in Haiti or Kuwait. I'm not
crying over you. It's this bitter
liquid I'm drinking,
flecked with wormwood,
that causes my sobbing.
That and the thought of a small
dog to whom I owe an apology.
If only I'd been born
a little earlier. I could've avoided
all the heartache you gave me,
and dated Amelia Earhart instead,
making salvation as well as
transatlantic plane flights attainable.
In this revised scenario, I'd never
even meet you (*my sulky twin,*
commander of battalions of beetles
who eat grievances like sweet potatoes)
due to my being inextricably linked
with the famous aviatrix.
The world would need to be remapped
under the circumstances, and history
rewritten, but all my sadness
would fit in a thimble or pillbox.

Continents would still drift,
but in far wiser directions. An
entirely new, improved universe
would be born, bereft of all our
sexual melancholy. In this rewriting
of my life, at bedtime I'd rest
my head on a thousand-pound book,
pages of arcane knowledge seeping
into my brain as I dozed. The toaster,
shelves and desk would be glazed
with a thin, glittery snow.
My presleep mind would never again
be battered by endless waves
of dread. Rather, Amelia's leather
goggles slung around my neck, I'd trace
flight patterns all night, and with
each breath exhale not exhaust fumes
but the comforting aroma of burnt donuts.

PRESCRIPTION FOR LIVING

It says here in today's paper
that a woman walked into the forest
and pierced a deer's ears so the creature
could wear her pearl earrings.
She felt the white-rumped doe
was woefully underdressed. Ah, humans.
How to explain them to you, my squalling
bald godchild, pleasing being
whose eyes comprise a watery paradise
the blue of petunias? I'm in no position
to give advice. If, by this incessant crying,
you insist, then listen: Visit the sick. Love
from a safe distance. Use high-powered
binoculars to view the temple roofs.
Never leave home without a rope ladder.
Sugared nuts in paper cups are fine to eat
when traveling. Avoid unfeeling thugs.
Don't imitate me and get weak-kneed
over every lad or lassie with a badass
vocabulary. You may embrace
the mysteries of Egyptian literature
at will. *Groan. Sigh.* This is a formal complaint,
a foghorn's refrain, a rainy day
statement dripped onto paper
I should chew up like spinach leaves
if I had any sense left after my recent arrest
for smuggling sheet music
into poorly orchestrated villages.
Comparisons between printed gift wrap
and the hairy hide of one's beloved

come much later, after the dish
in question has marinated for days
in strong beef broth and gets liberally
smeared with walnut paste. Did I mention
this missive's addressed to a baby,
eight days old, not yet addicted
to inhaling fossilized pollen
or bitten with cynicism?
Two huge hands part his curtains
each day as he wakes,
alarmingly early, his toys already
chattering in their soft patois.
That rectangular lily pond
in your backyard is classical in feeling.
You'll soon see what I mean.
Infant king, don't breathe a word
till you're ready, till spring's first purple
pansies are strewn in perfect ovals
round your crib, till it's been satisfactorily
explained to you why some of the dying
wail and buck and pound the walls
beside their beds, while others
return so meekly from whence they came.

To My Husband, on the First Anniversary of His Mother's Death

She still whirls through my mind
at a hundred miles an hour,
like the memory of a hurricane
survived as a child.
I never doubted her fury
could uproot telephone poles,
lift milk cows aloft, then
set them down gently, mooing,
acres away; or crumple and splinter
houses like cheap toys.
My tie to her was a binding one:
we were rivals. She made that clear
right away. Her end steeped you
in grief, battered your belief
in the universe as tender
and benevolent. She sank,
and the good earth swallowed
her—whether to crown her empress
of some underworld (she adored
and envied royalty), or to liberate
her from pain, or to feed trees
and enrich mineral deposits—
it doesn't much matter.
You were robbed of what formed you
and comprehended you best.
You spent last year skiing
in plaid pajamas, distracted,
depressed. The only member
of your family who possessed,

as you do, a geyser-like spirit
and a five alarm mind,
was silenced, suddenly
becoming geology, patiently
awaiting her headstone's
unveiling. Ever since you swam
out of her body on a river
of birth muck and blood,
this bond existed. If foolish
obstetricians thought for a moment
they'd severed you two
with the snip of a sterilized
scissor—well, what's a cut cord
between kindred affinities?
Her volcanic imaginings,
her genius for cursing a purgative
blue streak, these traits
are refined into literature in you.
All its life her turbulent mind
harbored death-grip obsessions:
with Nazis and their victims,
violence and crime, fears
of being smothered
by some sexual avalanche.
On good behavior she could charm
like a starlet. I'll always
be grateful to her for turning
a blind eye at the right moment,
allowing us to sneak off and marry.
She loved you, her only son,
desperately, comically,
jealously. She placed you
in the center of her spiraling

winds, right at the heart
of the odd calm at her storm's core.
There you remain, to this day,
protected, enclosed. She cannot
desert you or cease to surround you.
And I can do nothing but continue
to love you, with her grudging
permission.

A Sage in Retirement

Still more remote, the time
will arrive when we must surrender
ourselves to the binder of wounds
to be trussed up. Perish
that thought. Banish it to Africa.
Let it be rocked to sleep
in civilization's cradle.
He starts up from his humble bed
as if hearing a voice intoning
some private joke or an audience
chortling loudly afterwards.
You must consider the properties
of the waters, for they differ
in taste and weight. He's full
of electromagnetism and theories
about light particles. Women can't keep
their hands off him. *I am afflicted,*
he yawns, *with a sacred disease.* Actually,
he suffers from sciatica. He can barely
stir till well after dinner. People
claim to hear faint strains of music
in his presence, as though he were
an old radio, tuned down very low.

Spring Tonic

Clouds obscure the glory
   of your mornings, your pewter-plated
   afternoons, the fig trees of evening,
   alive with talkative birds.
It's been this way forever and a day.
This minute the air smells
like slug-colored medicines
you were given as a kid.
Childhood ought to be light-years
behind you, but isn't. Which old
terror or complaint seeps slow
as resin through your veins,
despite your gentle parents'
best efforts to purge it?
Your ragged spirit still flees you
so frequently: a mongrel slinking out
the dog-door of your mouth,
anxious to tip over trash cans,
chase vermin and get dirty
before limping home. What made you
furtive so early, amused only when horses
broke loose in the park and trampled
several church picnics,
or on the morning after Grandpa's
citrus groves froze in an ice storm?
Your mental weather's perpetually
inclement, like those dank fogs
once believed to be the breath
of disease. Only a meteorologist

could log your thoughts: *sea smoke,*
coronas, buttermilk billows.

This spring's uncertain currents
waft you back to the past, where
Mother and Father, huge painted
saints wearing paper crowns,
hold court in the dark, wielding
red-tipped cigarettes like scepters.
No one knew what was wrong with you.
You were fed thick medicinal liquids
whose sugary tinge failed
to disguise their chemical agendas.
Your tongue curled, a pink newborn
marsupial, afraid of the taste
of iron mixed with ink, or chalk thinned
with motor oil, or greasy silt left
in the pan after Mother fried liver.
Weren't those old potions meant
to cure everything: your sullenness
and tyrannical attachments;
your refusals to eat or speak;
and most of all the terrible religions
you kept inventing, which left you
hollow and rigid as some insect's
shed exoskeleton, ever meditating
on what it would be like
after you died and your body
TURNED INTO A WORM FARM.
No other thoughts fit in your head.
During those sickened nights
and glazed days, you never imagined
your *metamorphosis* (a word

you wouldn't learn for years)
might transform you into something
less like Mom's teeming compost heap—
and more enduring and bright,
like diamond.

CUT-UP

This peculiar ability of my giant dog
to shell and eat pistachio nuts,
to debate great apes at the National Zoo
and deny various tribes of aborigines;
to perpetuate the ornamental breeds,
resort to magic uniforms and to chew
grilled pork is not too pretty, but it is
a way of life and I am used to it by now.

July 3rd

Overcast till 4 P.M. Gunshot-like crackling
punctuates the hazy afternoon—
premature fireworks as neighbors
prepare earsplitting festivities
in honor of Independence Day.
Bees big as doorknobs buzz drunkenly by,
barely able to remain airborne.
The dog races ahead through Elysian
Park. We're on a dirt trail that winds
through California scrub—scorched hillsides
of orange nasturtiums,
morning glories colonizing small trees,
trunks unreadably graffitied in blue.
Blooming yellow anise, pepper trees
and parched jade plants. Scrolled
white jimson flowers jut up, ready
to unfurl like small torahs and reveal
their stern laws: *eat me at your peril,*
heedless vision seeker, hungry infidel.
My beloved, short-legged dog has something
suspicious between her teeth. I can tell
by the way she's holding it I'm going
to have to take it away from her—
it's some kind of contraband. She's thrilled
with her discovery, wants to eat whatever
it is right away. I have to tell her *drop*
that four or five times in a fake stern voice
before she obeys. It's a rodent torso—
a baby gopher or ground squirrel
from the waist up, tiny front limbs

all drawn in at the elbows, and the delicate
claws resemble a wren's. Its straight, yellow
buckteeth form the perfect gardening tool,
extending past the end of its whiskered chin.
The poor half-gopher's all dried out
by our desert weather. And I'm being mean
to deny the dog her treat, her fur-covered
meat prune. I tell myself I'm worried
about what the gopher died of—maybe
it'd make the dog sick, though most likely
the rodent's life ended from being chewed
in two, rather than some imagined
mammal plague I fret could harm my hound.
She regards me for a moment with tolerant
disdain, then trots off to sniff a beetle.
Black as a bobby pin, its shellacked butt
for some reason (mating stance?
insect religion?) is thrust up in the air.

I follow the dog, convinced
of her superior wisdom. She paws
a puckered patch of mud,
almost tromps on a wooly caterpillar.
Another firecracker whistles and booms.
She'll take on rattlesnakes or pit bulls
without hesitation but really fears
these explosions. Last Fourth of July,
skyrocket noises got her so riled
she chewed the wooden blinds
to splinters and gnawed off part
of a table leg. When I returned
from barbecuing, I found her
crammed under my desk, shivering.

Normally, she's so stoic. A book
I've read only parts of says that
in Greece, around 300 B.C., the Stoics
believed nothing could happen
which was not part of nature's
perfection. Man's duty was to
cheerfully accept whatever occurred,
secure in the knowledge it was all
for the best. If you traveled to Egypt
and a Nile crocodile bit your first-
born in twain, or the oracle at Delphi
prophesied ruin for you and your issue,
or your daughter got leprosy, or your son
was enslaved and made to wait upon foreign
heads of state naked, or your wife ran off
with five illiterate monks you'd paid
to stomp your grapes into wine, you were
supposed to remain calm, unmoved by good
fortune or bad, beyond hope or fear.

After you died, little brother, people
offered condolences. Since you're with me
now every second, you accompany the dog
and me on this hike. Sometimes, to be kind,
friends gently suggested that since you'd been
so ill, maybe it was better you'd passed into
infinity, where out-of-the-body adventures
commence. Maybe it was for the best, they said:
you'd graduated to ash and thus your sufferings
had ended. I admire those Stoics, truly I do:
their attempt to relish every strange fate
the earth serves up; their faith in nature—
that seizure-prone, sexy, bloodthirsty girl.

I comb the dog's fur with my fingers,
picking out foxtails. I find a clod of dirt
sprouting nine kinds of grass and give it a kick.
When a lifetime finishes, proteins fold
themselves into useful shapes, like clothes
neatly stored in drawers for future use.
Then the devout, clannish Stoics
clap their nonexistent hands, and the applause
is just deafening. *Bravo*, they yell, jumping
up and down. They pound the red velvet arms
of their chairs, wad up their programs and pelt
the stage with them. *More, more, more*, they chant,
faces hot, eyes brimming. *Let us hurtle through
the world again. We demand an encore.*

Address to a Broom

Away with your homely reproaches, you rough bundle of straw, wispy as the blond mustache just visible above Mother's upper lip. I conjured you to brush my sins into neat piles, to do my chores for me, soothe the floorboards my cruel boots misuse. But what sweeps clean also shoves dirt under the rug. You make flurries of all that has fallen, what should be left to settle unmolested and decompose into grit: hairs from heads I'd best forget, snippets of incriminating twine, skin flakes sloughed off the hides of fair-weather friends, petals dropped by bruised corsages, crumbs tumbled from indiscreet meals. Broom, you long, spindly arm that collars us slobs; you're the shifty janitor's right hand, a witch's steed, the neglected housewife's fox-trot partner, a scarecrow's backbone, the hyperactive first grader's unbloodied sword. What did I unleash when I unlocked your closet? Which magic words must I mumble to put a stop to you? *Dustbin, cookie tin, silver pin, can't win.* Too many brooms sweeping at once, scores of oars rowing me toward desert islands swiped clean of sand. Broom, you and your smug, wet-headed cousins the mops must halt this whisking industry. Quit fingering my debris. Abandon your flat-footed accomplice the dustpan. No more of your stiff justice, your rigid peasant cleanliness, you poker of cobwebs, destroyer of the nests of honest wasps. You're a ragged bird's nest lashed to a branch, a poor impersonation of a bouquet. I'd sooner lick up what sullies the linoleum each day than listen to your faint, scraping accusations or your bristly whispering ever again.

THE HOLY STORM

(A SECULAR SNOW SERMON)

Howling is the noise of hell, singing the voice of heaven.
—John Donne

*After the snowstorms come avalanches, varying greatly in
form, size, behavior and in the songs they sing . . .*
—John Muir

Snow is a miracle. It takes its place among earth's endless cavalcade of
amazements: giraffes, tears, neurotransmitters. Pastrami sandwiches, armadillos, kissing. Snow's holiness holds true regardless of your, or my,
personal views on the etiology of the miraculous. Whether you believe
Nature's wonders resulted from spontaneous combustion or from the
blueprints of an overworked, lonely, chain-smoking supreme being;
or from the collaborative efforts of a giddy cast of divinities clad in
togas, thongs or clingy silver space suits; it's difficult to find a human
without some reservoir of awe for what could be the thumbprint of *some-
body's* lord, or just winter's white signature—this delicate yet mighty
landscape-shaping precipitation.

Parallel proverbs from several countries cite the positive, generative effects of snow on the earth itself. "A snow year, a rich year." "Snow which
lies fattens the ground." "Under water, famine; under snow, bread." The
folk wisdom seems to be that snow is heavenly compost, placating and
nourishing the hungry earth. It can have similar effects on us.

Like flurries of tiny stars, snow accents both our largeness and our insignificance. We need a microscope to completely appreciate snowflakes,
their lovely crystalline forms: chiseled mineral sunbursts the size of pinheads, as idiosyncratic as we are. Snow melts in our hands but will also

outlast us. Thus snow encourages meditation on the eternal and the ephemeral.

Snow descends from the clouds, where some have thought they discerned intimations of paradise's skyline. But whatever its ultimate origin, we must be deeply grateful that the snow stoops to fraternize with us mortals. It clings to the earth, our trodden element, constructing its own cold, lumpy temples among us, on roofs and roads, in lake beds and low-lying meadows. It frosts and temporarily redesigns our buildings. It reroutes traffic for a while, lest we forget we live at the mercy of forces that dwarf us. Snow blesses us with its shifting, ethereal presence while we sit in front of the fire, scratching ourselves nervously and fretting about God and His perceived absences and slights, torturing ourselves about other issues entirely, or perhaps luxuriating in the certainty of His love. As St. Francis preached to the birds, calling them his little sisters, he admonished them to "always and in every place" praise God, for many reasons, including that birds are "beholden to Him for the element of the air which He hath appointed to you. . . ." In a similar spirit, we must be grateful, both chill-embracing skiers and wimpy shiverers alike, for the glistening astonishment of winter and its generous harvests of snow. The snow envelops, replenishes, bandages, adorns, *becomes* our element, during its irregularly scheduled visits.

Snow falls on us so soundlessly. Humans sorely need intermittent silences, which can soothe like fragrant balm. Howard Chandler Robbins wrote: "There is something solemnizing and restful in this quietness of nature, something that for our soul's growth and good we need to take into our consciousness." There is no richer, more fulfilling quiet than a windless snow that begins to fall just as dusk is pinkening the windows. That's one example of the soundless way snow sings. Humans crave water and beauty, among other things. Many of us secretly treasure hopes of being reformed. Snow feeds these longings and more. It assists us in our constant struggles to attain patience, peace and islands of delight.

THINGS THAT LOOSEN THE TONGUE

The sight of a drowned child.
A swallow of whitewash.
The sound of dogs cracking
marrow bones with their wise
incisors. Walrus cutlets
for lunch. A scream
turned to wood smoke
in her throat. An expanse
of starry flowers. Winter
ravenousness. Having your head
pelted with rotten persimmons.
Dust-flavored tequila
sipped from a thimble.
Hearing sneezes under your bed
and finding the bicycle repairman
trembling there. Off-color jokes.
The faint, toxic scent of mothballs.
Whooping cough. A jail sentence.
A group of nudes in a wooded landscape
fingering soft wooly foliage.

WORD SALAD

Sheriffs, lepers, shy denizens
of the twelfth century; harlots,
charlatans, bunglers, and horse thieves;
all those with unstained maiden names,
repeat after me. Trees releaf,
their roots drink up the earth's wild gripes.
Bewitched opticians sob with grief,
wetting their endive bow ties, crowns
of celery sadly askew.
Usherettes, cuckoo clock carvers,
furriers: by your instructions
we come to know gardening's art.
Ravioli makers, swindlers,
busybodies and parlor snakes:
we are moved to say mass over
this salad, so licorice-y
are its greens. Snapdragons wilt quick.
But a chiffonaide of beet leaves
maintains its flat adoration
even of those who'd do it harm.
Hence, such weak ingredients must
be coddled, kissed, washed in shrew's milk.
Pharaohs, feral babes, farmers' wives,
you persecuted Jewesses:
tell me the truth. Grass clings to earth,
so devoted. Will you come to
know me by nibbling my stalk?
When she hit me in the face with
her tomato bouquet, I knew,
lickety split, that from among

the thousands of alert girls I
put through their paces every day
I could love only her, with those
well-sucked, asparagus-colored
thumbs. Meanwhile, I tried the manners
of a rude schoolboy on for size
and felt well pleased with the results.
I expect she'll get this passage
memorized by Friday and that
by Sunday I'll have her knocked up.
Then she'll eat peas and curled ferns till
the doctor tells her not to, or
until she gets a phone message
from the emperor, whose ninety-
nine bright-eyed concubines ply him
with aphrodisiac snacks like rice
wine, prunes that are so popular
in brothels, red rooster pills and
wolfberries. The berries work quite
well, as she and I both know. Their
one small drawback is that they tend
to turn the eater's drool dark blue.

MYSTERIOUS TEARS

A homicide detective has the grave responsibility of resolving
the most serious criminal act one human can commit against another.
Therefore, we bear an important burden when called upon
to investigate a death, for we stand in the dead person's shoes,
so to speak, to protect his or her interests against everybody else's.

We're lucky she was killed in snow. This kind of old, crumbly
snow's impressionable. Her January garden. Pathetic.
Shows she had a soft spot for lost causes: winter gardening
at this elevation, and that Dutchman. He's handsome.
I'll give him that. He'll be Miss Popularity in prison.
Look. There're deer footprints all over. Plants nibbled
to nubs—a real deer cafeteria. Remember that case
with an African parrot as sole witness? "Don't, please don't!"
is all it kept screaming. Talking birds freak me out.
I wouldn't let my partner leave me alone with it.
I'd be more comfortable hearing a beer can or matchbook speak.
Snapped-off prairie grass: sure sign of a fight.

The Dutchman lies on his back in the holding cell,
complaining to the ceiling "I'm starved! When do we eat?,"
eyes hot with mysterious tears. He's got such a mob yelling
in his head, voices from various centuries—Calamity Jane,
Job, one of Hitler's assistants, that little boy from the *Lassie*
TV show. He probably can't remember which one convinced
him to kill her. Maybe they ganged up on him.

Till each crime's solved I carry a postmortem Polaroid
of the victim's face in my wallet—which has gotten a lot

fatter than I'd like. Pictures of my kids I keep in a different
compartment, back here, with the cash.

Nestled in the crotch of this dwarf tree: an unexpected find.
A nest and five bluish eggs scrawled with tiny purple
hieroglyphics. My wife, one of the happy fraternity of naturalists,
would know how to read these. I'm stumped. Slate-colored
junco or common nighthawk? Perhaps an olive-backed thrush.
More witnesses who won't talk. That includes you, too,
bloodstained leather gardening gloves, iron gate, dead vines,
and worms curling and uncurling where we dug them up,
like infants' fingers.

If the photographer's all through, let the dogs loose
inside the hedge border awhile. Maybe they can sniff out
some underpinnings and not just piss all over the crime scene,
like last time.

My wife says no dwelling has more integrity than a well-made nest.

Our search should begin in the area immediately surrounding
the body and proceed outward.

Apparently all he's done since his arrest is cry.
Did the beefy Dutchman weep as he stabbed her,
watched by these primitive winter roses?

The badly scratched victim still brandishes a fork.
Bits of heavily peppered egg cling to the tines.
I think I saw a wound on the back of the Dutchman's
hand that looked like a fork-stab: four tiny holes. Let's check.
Looks like she tried to defend herself with a trowel, too.

She should have smashed him on the skull with the shovel.
It was right there, in arm's reach. I don't think mammals
should die with their eyes open, do you? Blood gets fanned out
around the neck kind of capelike, due to arterial gushing.
Don't step in it! Blood's more slippery than ice. You don't
want to fall on your ass and ruin that suit. Looks new.
Little tangles of dark hair, just what might be caught
in her comb some morning, skitter between the tree roots
like shy spiders. Bet you twenty bucks some of her black hair
ends up lining a bird's nest next spring.

RETREAT

How do trees grieve?
Clichés tell us
the doubled-over willow
weeps subtle tears
which flavor the lake
as her trailing branches
tickle its waters, grazing
the occasional drowned hand.
Perhaps this stand of liquid amber
inwardly wilts as adult trees sway
above hacked saplings,
mauled shrubs, trampled grasses—
I've told that gardener
more than once he's got
a butcher's handshake.
Ancient, headstrong elms
drool clear juices
humans aren't astute enough
to transfuse,
after tree surgeons
ignorant of trunk or leaf anesthesia
perform chainsaw amputations.
Ever sensitive, the soul
of a broad-leafed maple
felled for veneer sleeps
fitfully within my coffee table.
Once its cells ate light
and manufactured green sweetness.
I grip this fork, napkin in my lap,
daunted by wronged objects.

This enraged vase. The sawtoothed
spirit gleaming in my grapefruit spoon.
I can't even have breakfast
without laying waste. It's my
nature. Grain ground to flour,
molded into loaves
for toast: forgive me.
We never learned to tread gently.
Now our dwindling joys
are mass-produced or imagined.
Stolen clothes muffle us,
cloaks and turbans mask
our earthy scents. *Travel by camel.*
Subsist on bacon drippings. Do no harm.
The bamboo bench thirsts and creaks
at floodtime. So do I,
though for the past several generations
I've been editing my amends:
this many-paged treatise
on the color of seawater.

MEDICINE

Are we saviors or sadists? the young doctor asks
as he anoints himself with his favorite aftershave.
Its name means "effervescent saliva" in French. Brains
sit in liquid-filled jars on his polished mahogany
desktop. Lopped-off fingers and toes lie in cheesecloth-
covered beakers on tiered metal shelves, chains
of bubbles snaking up from under the nails. Bluish babies,
who never drew breath, are preserved in honey-
colored solutions, eyelids thin as sweet-pea petals,
hands balled into fists the size of apricot pits.
Their unspent lives represent heaven's necessary
percentage of errors. *One sees here so clearly,*
the physician whispers, tapping the glass behind
which one stunted infant swims, *what a flimsy
garment the flesh is.*

You must have sex immediately after drinking
this elixir if you want it to work. Then, very
carefully, inoculate yourself with the tip of this
porcupine quill. When the sand in your hourglass
runs out, skim this slim volume on the history
of quicksilver. Guaranteed to cure fits,
biliousness and the shivers.

Our wants are modest. Nights, we crave unbroken
sleep. Daily, we seek mind-bending pleasures
that erase, then remake the world in new,
scintillating rhythms and tints, with a dose
more poetry than it seemed to conceal before.
We need our crocodile bites healed immediately,

our achy joints oiled. We pray hot, hissing
liquids never drip from our ears, not even
in dreams. We demand protection against sweaty
feet, bladder gravel, fermenting breath. Mix me
a tincture this instant to make the baby
stop crying. Use opium, snuff, dove's blood,
anything! A house call in winter means hitch up
the snorting horse and fill the carriage
with blankets. He reads my secretions,
even deciphers the sign some mute god
scrawled on the nape of my neck. But I won't let
anyone cut windows into me and expose
what I'm bloated with: caviar, grass fires
and ambergris. Three-foot-high pianists
adorned with orchids, and a bunch
of other stuff that looks like sushi.

An individual's vigilance has broken down.
Yellow fever, sleeping sickness, typhus,
anthrax. A girl insulted a demon; slighted
the whiny spirit of a mosquito-breeding
stream; transgressed by playing games
with her siblings at the foot of a vindictive
tree. Polio, dysentery, malaria, pox, cholera.
We must bury seven lemons, three pieces
of broomstick and a fish's vertebrae
in order to restore her.

I've drunk the birdbath water and licked
a leather Bible cooked in oil. I've crushed
hogs' teeth into my tea. I've rinsed my hair
in the tin basin a genius has spat in. This
morning, after being washed and dressed

66

by orphans, I drank the iridescent vinegar
pearls were dissolved in, which you so kindly
provided. But I'm getting sick of these
prescriptions. I wish to be repaired, quickly
and completely, little and piteous though I am.

It was my sister's touch
that healed him as much
as the dozen jellied ducks'
tongues he ingested.

This illness is a flight from something.
Cease to flee. Turn and face what pursues
you. Conquer and thrive. Change with each
season. Molt. Evolve. Mutate. Rail. Your
enemies will shrivel and wail, fester and lament.
Something has trespassed in your temple, barged
into your tent, infected your cellar full of tightly
corked wine bottles. It wanders your byways,
lighting cooking fires, hunting, gouging its initials
into the trunks of your forests. Think back
on what's traveled in and out of you in recent weeks.
Whose rice have you eaten? Whose tongue have you
sucked? Cheese is not a bad food, just toxic under
certain conditions, if eaten thoughtlessly at unlucky
times. Wine can be mischievous. Inventory your
organs. Interrogate your skeleton. You were saying
good-bye to someone, but agreed to meet him again
before long. Now that's not possible. He's too ill
to remember your name. You were on your way
to make charcoal. You'd gone after a cow that had
wandered off. You were skimming vats of goat cheese,
picking the kids up at day care or phoning your broker.

You suffer from numbness, obstructions, loss of heat,
fevers, rumblings in the chest and bowels. Now someone
is weeping on the other side of your door. To appear
after one's death in front of one's children, strong
and undefiled—who wouldn't wish for this
impossibility? Meanwhile, you fret at the mirror,
prod your sagging chin, yank the flesh tight
under your eyes, glimpsing the magic a plastic
surgeon might perform for a small fortune.
Your hair is thinning. Your complexion becomes
a map of your travels. Chew these peach leaves,
curved like scythe blades. Hailstorms pelt us
with millions of pills. You'd be cured if you could
tempt a crow, one of those swaggering birds
you love so much, to nest on your head.

Gulp dust scraped from the face of a statue—
a naval hero guarding a large public park
is best. Inhale a pinch of the mold
that grows in the holds of wooden ships.
Wear a dog's hide for a week. Just see if you
don't feel better the moment you slip
the itchy thing off. Say "Sit still, my soul,
no more growing sour," at least five thousand times.
Drink sycamore milk a mouse tail has soaked in.
The syrup in this dropper-capped bottle contains
rattlesnake meat plus sixty other ingredients.

Latin sounds formal and creaky as our monastery's
wrought-iron doors. Hepatitis, hemophilia,
influenza. These terrors that infest us
have been given labels ornate as maidens'
Christian names. Leukemia. Diphtheria.

Diseases, too, are living things, driven,
as we are, to find homes, to be fruitful and multiply.
Let me sleep on the church floor where
harm dare not enter. The priest promises
he will treat me. He says sunlight
and fierce, shouted prayer to get God's
attention are the best disinfectants.
His white beard, which he occasionally braids,
is twisted into two tails—the beautiful
shape of the root of a tooth.

She leapt out of her sickbed and ran to me, having thrown
away her crutches. It was quite a sight, as nightgowns
were not in use during that era. My wooden leg
disinclined me to dance with her, much as I liked
the way she smelled—like brioche and pump water.

We're oddly composed, the young doctor thinks,
knotting his tie. *We're tender and digestible.*
Teeth, those broken pillars, whose rude eruption
through the gums causes infants such exquisite
discomfort. The skull, a snifter in which decades
of shipwrecked thoughts fizz. Then there's digestion's
wretched complexity, our sex organs' inopportune
simpering, the skin's tell-all topography. Why wouldn't
she take an innocent glass of wine with me? he frets.
Do I reek of formaldehyde? He pats on more
aftershave, till an invisible cloud of aroma
surrounds him. *We're ambling bags of juice and gas,*
wafting in and out of consciousness, he decides
for the millionth time. *We read, breed, hope rarebit's*
on tonight's menu, consult our watches. He realizes
he's late. *Oh, the infernos we fancy we contain*

till we get emptied into infinity, he says out loud,
proud of the sound of his pronouncement.
The educated, nasal twang of his voice is thrilling
enough but it does not comfort him. Annoyed
at having misplaced yet another cuff link, he kisses
the tip of his pinky and presses it against the cool,
dusty side of the nearest baby-containing jar.
"Be safe, darling," he murmurs, grabbing his coat
and shouldering open the door.

A Crushed House

Three days of storms. Snow
coats tree branches, blankets
roofs and the road, padding
this part of the planet
so we can't touch our boots to
that stubborn brown clay
we're all sculpted from.
Why weren't we formed of snow—
a more wind-borne, ethereal material?
Dogs, ecstatic after the heavy snow,
crest piles and dive in, dig tunnels,
bore holes in its crust
with hot spurts of urine.
Soundless, gritty white whirlwinds
kick up in the distance. You can ski
down the street. A monster tree
snapped in half last night
and crushed a house four doors
down. Luckily, the owners
had gone south for Christmas.
This morning you can see
right inside. Framed woodcuts
in the front room. A lamp
bent over a small table
as though closely examining it.
A shelf holding up baskets
of potted plants. The township
posted a notice on the battered house,
which the wind rescinded.
Snow's piled higher than the top

of the front door frame. The dog
shows me how easily you can climb
a heap of snow, then walk right
into the second story
and mess around in the house.
I told her we had to be content
with looking in. This is part of our
bargain, our interspecies partnership:
she sniffs out what's fun, and I veto
her great ideas 99 times out of 100.
The pitched roof was partly glass,
like on a greenhouse. Its smashed
panes admit a jumble of fir branches,
splintered wood and choking mounds
of snow. It looks almost as though
the snow broke into the house
all by itself, and is slowly
filling it, like pounds and pounds
of sugar being forced down someone's
throat. Why is the sight of a
torn-open house so riveting?
I suppose humans like to look at
innards, the secret workings,
see where the plumbing and aortas
lead. Think of the house as a head
with a gaping cranial wound,
from which a thousand doubts
and cabin fever are streaming.
Inside the fractured wooden skull
the houseplants are having
a gradually fainter conversation
about how bitter the wind is.

CORPSE AND MOURNER

Corpse:
The free-floating grief I felt all my life
hung round my neck like a willow wreath.
Melancholy tripped me up, made me wear
its long nightshirt embroidered
with cornflowers. All I recognized
was seen through the prisonish grid
of my eyelashes. Had I died a century
earlier, they'd have lined my coffin
with nutgrass and butcher's broom—
mangy bed straw. This mahogany box
with brass fittings is nothing like
the ironed linens you and I grew
used to, but I lie quiet inside anyway.

A flock of ring-necked doves settles
on the synagogues's gravel roof,
to skitter and coo. Dandelions sprout
from the rain gutters. Doves
fly down to preen in the sun
and peck rice left over from weddings.
Unclench your thoughts. *Let me go.*

All rise, he sings, marigold wilting
in his lapel. For the American reader,
the blue prayer books will seem
written backwards. The service begins.
Afterwards, at the reception,
she won't eat, though everyone else,
particularly the children,

feed their faces.
Jews never miss an opportunity to berate
themselves, even at funerals. The synagogue
smells like dill. She sat as if asleep.
Unable to utter even a squeak.

Open your hands. Open your eyes.
I'm right here. The needs of the living
quickly pass on. Sunflowers, sleep herbs,
military orchids. Perhaps some asparagus.
Bless your slightly open lips, your yellow
teeth, the rasp of bread knives being sharpened
in the kitchen. And bless me, in most need
of blessing. Me, eater of crumbs.

Mourner:
I was dead wrong. I admit this, to the dirt
tossed atop his coffin. His nearness gave me
an itchy passion rash. Emotional poison ivy.
No lotion helped. I nearly perished
of embarrassment. His bitter distance
like a steady diet of sour melon
and raw leek, washed down with thistle beer.
The big colorful world whistles on
without him now and the whirligig
between my ears continues to spin
and dizzy me. If I cannot have you in my arms
then I'll retain you some other way.
You'll always occupy my mind. It's true.
He whose dark word brings on the night
left me his tape measure to reckon
the lengths of my days.

FUGITIVE COLOR

The fading valor of the past
flaunts its flaglike tints.
Your nut brown hair
abdicated to gray. Jane's
theatrical blushes, staining
face and neck raspberry, should
be included in this list
of diffident, short-lived
or semi-visible tints.
Also we must mention colors
leached by the sun from
billboards or hair ribbons.
She came to live with us
when her eyesight failed,
so all she'd seen—weather-beaten,
sketchy, or shocking pink—
retreated into the dim realm
of afterimage and aura.
Threadbare sheets and pillow slips
exchange brightness for gauzy
softness. Then there's the smeared,
jumpy blur I see when I shut my eyes
and try to read the dog's mind—
or the flickering souls of dinner plates
and doorknobs who're certain
they're monuments. A childish,
bright violet desire to cry is
scorched into drab, unvoiced joy

by the heat of the waffle iron,
which crimps the air in this kitchen,
where curtains stir like the surface
of some vanished river.

A Severe Lack of Holiday Spirit

I dread the icy white concussion
of winter. Each snowfall demands
panic, like a kidnapper's hand
clapped over my chapped mouth.
Ice forms everywhere, a plague
of glass. Christmas ornaments'
sickly tinkle makes my molars ache.
One pities the anemic sun
come January. Trees go skeletal.
Children born in the chilly months
are apt to stammer. People hit
the sauce in a big way all winter.
Amidst blizzards they wrestle
unsuccessfully with the dark comedy
of their lives, laughter trapped
in their frigid gizzards. Meanwhile,
the mercury just plummets,
like a migrating duck blasted
out of the sky by some hunter
in a cap with fur earflaps.

"THE LANDSCAPE SENDS US OUR BELOVED."

—WALTER BENJAMIN, *THE METAPHYSICS OF YOUTH*

Then let the land send a handpicked
man, a thick-stemmed lily. Will he
arrive drenched, having stepped
from the riverbed, gravel and rust
rumbling under his tongue? As noble
open as he is closed, as gorgeous
erect as he is wilted, sprung up
among flowering onions, scraped
aside by spades and rakes,
he has sown himself across acres
of forests and sacred lakeshores
in riotous drifts. His desires
whiten like milk thistle, like bones
picked clean by crows. During
the third week of his search for me,
he sits and rests against the trunks
of a hottentot fig and its sibling.
"Hey, two-legged being," they cry out,
"ignore the jewel weed's stupid crooning.
Quit chipping words into rocks.
Do something useful. Make it rain."

TIDINGS

I'm sorry to write you this news, as it is anything but encouraging . . .
   however, on the bright side:
the armless violinist Mom recommended has such a cheerful spirit!

The kind of man who can wax eloquent about sackcloth caftans, her
   5th husband
owns a flooded sulfur mine. He's insufferable, with his sick giggle and
   infinite chins.

Still, I urged her not to leave him. *Remember,* I said, *despite all, he is the
   father of your little girl.*
My beloved son in whom I am well pleased lies under a quilt of snow,
   mind vibrating.

*Let us put aside petty bickering and retrieve a few of these oboes and French
   horns floating downriver,*
she whispered to the minister as she let him in, wearing a silver dress
   that resembled a waterfall

I never liked your manner better toward me than when you kissed me
   last May.
A ladder appeared in my living room, and you climbed it up through
   the skylight and picked almonds for me.

He sat in the basement, rereading old newspapers. Then he went and
   stood all night under a tree,
while she lay on a low stone wall brooding about the fact that the
   spirits no longer speak to her.

Her elation seeing me again at the riverbank prayer meeting was
    mixed with ferocity.
This being so, it's a thousand pities I was not allowed to lick the
    petals' rosy edges.

Tell the combustible boy that when his bed-wetting problem is solved
    I will consider his proposal,
as I have finally learnt my lucky days, months and numbers by heart.

In honor of our arisen loved ones, the choir sang several appropriate
    selections,
then we all sat down to big plates of strawberry shortcake with gobs of
    whipped cream.

Amy, dear, don't know whose ghost is holding him captive? I'll give
    you a hint.
Her name starts with a "G" and she's feeding him bits of poppies and
    foxglove.

NIGHTFALL

Her ashes reside in a pale blue vase
her sister, a glassblower, blew. She died
at twenty-nine, several decades too early.
This body, now destroyed, dissolves in light.
Light is a solvent, the means by which
we're translated into another medium.
I could feel her rising a thousand times
during the service. A man in the pew
in front of me had a bad case of fungus
behind his right ear. I couldn't
help noticing. You cannot intercede
in his grief. There's a kind of wine
made from bones, someone said. Supposedly,
it tastes like milk. Bagpipes were played
at the graveside. But I digress.
A period of mourning has no definite
duration. Our search for what endures
continues. The fragrance of ink,
breasts freckled as pears, asses
that clench, jiggle and glow
like the animated planets they are.
Dinosaur remains full of unlaid eggs
have been dug up. An auctioneer
takes bids on a hank of Abe Lincoln's
hair. When the dead are well cared for,
they enter the earth and are happy.

About the Author

Amy Gerstler is a writer of fiction, poetry, and journalism, who lives in Los Angeles. Her eighth book, *Bitter Angel*, was published by North Point Press (1990), and was awarded a National Book Critics Circle Award in poetry in 1991. Her book *Crown of Weeds* won a California Book Award in 1998. Her previous seven books include *The True Bride* (Lapis Press, 1986) and *Primitive Man* (Hanuman Books, 1987). In 1987 she was awarded second place in *Mademoiselle* magazine's fiction contest. Her work has appeared in numerous magazines and anthologies, including *The Paris Review* and *The Best American Poetry*. Text works of hers have been performed at the Museum of Contemporary Art in Los Angeles, and elsewhere. In the fall of 1989, she collaborated on an installation at the Santa Monica Museum of Art, and a related artists' book, with visual artist Alexis Smith, both of which are titled *Past Lives*. The installation traveled to the Josh Baer Gallery in New York City in December 1990. She contributes reviews to *Artforum* magazine. Her writing has appeared in catalogs for exhibitions at the Long Beach Museum of Art, Los Angeles Contemporary Exhibitions, the Whitney Museum of American Art, the Los Angeles Museum of Contemporary Art, the Fort Wayne Museum of Art (Fort Wayne, Indiana), and Security Pacific Inc. She is a graduate adviser at Art Center College of Design in Pasadena, California, and teaches in the graduate writing program at Antioch West.

PENGUIN POETS

Ted Berrigan	*Selected Poems*
Philip Booth	*Pairs*
Jim Carroll	*Fear of Dreaming*
Jim Carroll	*Void of Course*
Nicholas Christopher	*5° & Other Poems*
Carl Dennis	*Ranking the Wishes*
Diane di Prima	*Loba*
Stuart Dischell	*Evenings & Avenues*
Stephen Dobyns	*Common Carnage*
Stephen Dobyns	*Pallbearers Envying the One Who Rides*
Paul Durcan	*A Snail in My Prime*
Amy Gerstler	*Crown of Weeds*
Amy Gerstler	*Medicine*
Amy Gerstler	*Nerve Storm*
Debora Greger	*Desert Fathers, Uranium Daughters*
Robert Hunter	*Glass Lunch*
Robert Hunter	*Sentinel*
Barbara Jordan	*Trace Elements*
Jack Kerouac	*Book of Blues*
Ann Lauterbach	*And For Example*
Ann Lauterbach	*On a Stair*
William Logan	*Night Battle*
William Logan	*Vain Empires*
Derek Mahon	*Selected Poems*
Michael McClure	*Huge Dreams: San Francisco and Beat Poems*
Michael McClure	*Three Poems*
Carol Muske	*An Octave Above Thunder*
Alice Notley	*The Descent of Alette*
Alice Notley	*Mysteries of Small Houses*
Lawrence Raad	*The Probable World*
Anne Waldman	*Kill or Cure*
Anne Waldman	*Marriage: A Sentence*
Rachel Wetzsteon	*Home and Away*
Philip Whalen	*Overtime: Selected Poems*
Robert Wrigley	*In the Bank of Beautiful Sins*
Robert Wrigley	*Reign of Snakes*